Table of Contents

Table of Contents 2

Introduction 4

Structure of the Seder 5

The Seder Plate 6

The 15 Steps of the Seder 7

סימני הסדר 7

Kadesh: Sanctifying Time 8

Urchatz 9

Karpas 10

Yachatz 11

Maggid 12

Four Questions 13

Storytelling: Multiple Options 14

A Passover Skit 16

The Four Children 17

Standing Up for Us 20

'Arami Oved Avi' 20

The Ten Plagues 21

Dayeinu 23

Pesach, Matzah and Maror 24

In Every Generation 26

Toast for completing Maggid 27

Hallel: Psalm 13 28

2nd Cup 29

Rachtzah 30

Motzi Matzahh 31

Maror 32

Khorech 33

Sulchan Orech 34

Eating the Hidden Afikoman 35

Bircat Hamazon 36

Third Cup of Wine 36

Cup of Elijah 37

Fourth Cup of Wine 38

Nirtza 41

Introduction

Through the years I have attended many different Seders. I have partaken in Seders in the east, the west and even in Israel. Each family carried with it their own traditions and customs in how a Seder was run. The one unifying theme through all the Seders was that they utilized generic Haggadot – maybe not the same one, but a basic one purchased in a store as it was the one available. Regardless of location, there was always an aspect of the Seder that never made sense to me – why are we doing this? Is this the next step? What are we even doing?

So, I decided I wanted to create a Haggadah that somehow brings more meaning to the Seder process. We often get so bogged down in reading the words, that the meaning of the entire evening is lost.

In the pages to follow, I have compiled what I considered are the essentials for prayer, but I have tried to accompany them with explanations, instructions, and food for thought in hopes that it will dispel with some of the difficulty in both understanding what we are doing as well as why we are doing it.

Ideally, each person at the Seder table would have a copy of this Haggadah in their hands so that they can read the explanations, and join in prayer. I have included the Hebrew, the transliterations, as well as the translations for all the prayers.

Fortunately, this is a work in progress. I expect to continue to edit this as we move forward through the years, and each year be able to only better the functionality and use of this Haggadah. I have no formal religious training, so I am certain there is room for improvement. If you catch any errors, typos, omissions or simply have a suggestion please let me know. I had created this for my own family, and after some years and prodding from family, decided to make it publicly available.

Structure of the Seder

The Seder is essentially structured around four cups of wine with one for good luck (i.e. Elijah's cup). The four cups of wine that are consumed during the seder are meant to represent the four expressions of redemption that are mentioned in the Torah in connection with the Passover story:

The four cups of wine that are a central part of the Passover seder are an important symbol of the liberation of the Israelites from slavery in ancient Egypt. According to the Torah, when God brought the ten plagues upon Pharaoh and the Egyptians, he instructed the Israelites to mark their doorposts with the blood of a sacrificed lamb so that their firstborn children would be spared. The Israelites were also told to eat a special meal in haste, with their clothing belted, their staff in hand, and their shoes on their feet. This meal, which was held on the eve of the Exodus, is the basis for the Passover seder.

First Cup: 'Kadesh'
The evening opens with The first cup, called the Cup of Sanctification. It is filled and blessed at the beginning of the seder. It is a symbol of the Kiddush, a blessing over wine that is recited at the start of the seder and that sanctifies the holiday of Passover.

Second Cup: 'Maggid'
The second cup, called the Cup of Plagues, is filled and consumed after the recitation of the Ten Plagues during the Maggid (telling of the Passover story). It is a symbol of the plagues that God brought upon Pharaoh and the Egyptians as a way of compelling them to free the Israelites.

Third Cup: 'Shulchan Orech'
The third cup, called the Cup of Redemption, is filled and consumed after the meal, at the end of the seder. It is a symbol of the redemption of the Israelites from slavery in Egypt.

Elijah's Cup:
After dinner an extra cup is poured in honor of Elijah and the door is opened to welcome the messianic age.

Fourth Cup: 'Hallel'
The fourth cup, called the Cup of Praise, is filled and consumed after the recitation of the Hallel (Psalms of praise). It is a symbol of the praise and thanksgiving that is offered to God for the redemption of the Israelites.

Concluding Songs
The famous folksongs like "Chad Gadya" constitute a medieval appendix to the Rabbinic four cup structure.

The Seder Plate

The Passover Seder plate is a special plate that is used during the Passover seder to hold a number of symbolic foods. Each of these foods has a specific meaning and represents a different aspect of the Passover story and the liberation of the Israelites from slavery in ancient Egypt

Maror – The bitter herb. To remind us of the bitterness of the slavery of our forefathers in Egypt.

Charoset – A mix of sweet wine, apples, cinnamon and nuts that resembles the mortar used as bricks of the many buildings the Jewish slaves built in Egypt.

Karpas – A reminder of the backbreaking work of the Jews as slaves.

Zeroah – represents the lamb that was the special paschal sacrifice on the eve of the exodus from Egypt.

Beitzah – The egg symbolizes the pre-holiday offering that was brought in the days of the Holy Temple.

The 15 Steps of the Seder

סימני הסדר

In the Temple Days, the spiritual pilgrimage reached its climax at the 15 stairs leading up to the Holy of Holies. The Signposts of the Seders, in turn are symbolized by 15 steps to the Seder.

Kadesh	Recitation of the Kiddush: blessing over 1st cup of wine.
UrChatz	First Handwashing (_without_ a blessing)
Karpas	First Dipping: Vegetable and Salt water
Yachatz	Breaking the Middle Matzah
Maggid	Storytelling: Exodus and etc. (longest part of Seder)
Rachtza	Second Handwashing (_with_ a blessing)
Motzi	First blessing over the matzah and the meal
Matzah	Eating of the Matzah with an emphasis about Matzah as a ritual of Passover
Maror	Second dipping: Eating of the bitter herbs
Korech	Eating of the Hillel sandwich (Matzah and maror)
Sulchan Orech	Eating of the festive meal (aka Dinner)
Tzafun	Eating the Afikomen (the last thing you eat tonight)
Barech	Birkat hamazon (the blessing after eating)
Hallel	Singing Psalms of Praise
Nirtza	Concluding prayers and folk songs

This Haggadah will have a progress bar at the top of each page denoting our progress through the 15 steps of the Seder, in order to help make it clear how it all comes together.

Kadesh: Sanctifying Time

The Kiddush sanctifies not the wine, but the holiday. Pesach is dedicated "to remember the Day of your Exodus from Egypt." (Ex.13:3)

Stand to recite the Kiddush, then **recline** to the left to drink the wine as befits nobles.

בָּרוּךְ אַתָּה יי אלהינו מֶלֶךְ הָעוֹלָם בּוֹרֵא פְּרִי הַגָּפֶן.

Baruch atah Adonai, Eloheinu melech ha'olam, borei p'ri hagafen.

Praised are you, Lord our God, Ruler of the universe, who has created the fruit of the vine.

בָּרוּךְ אַתָּהיי אלוהינו מֶלֶךְ הָעוֹלָם, אֲשֶׁר בָּחַר בָּנוּ מִכָּל עָם וְרוֹמְמָנוּ מִכָּל לָשׁוֹן וְקִדְּשָׁנוּ בְּמִצְוֹתָיו. וַתִּתֶּן לָנוּ אַהֲבָה מוֹעֲדִים לְשִׂמְחָה, חַגִּים וּזְמַנִּים לְשָׂשׂוֹן, אֶת יוֹם חַג הַמַּצּוֹת הַזֶּה, זְמַן חֵרוּתֵנוּ, מִקְרָא קֹדֶשׁ, זֵכֶר לִיצִיאַת מִצְרָיִם. כִּי בָנוּ בָחַרְתָּ וְאוֹתָנוּ קִדַּשְׁתָּ מִכָּל הָעַמִּים, וּמוֹעֲדֵי קָדְשֶׁךָ בְּשִׂמְחָה וּבְשָׂשׂוֹן הִנְחַלְתָּנוּ. בָּרוּךְ אַתָּה יי, מְקַדֵּשׁ יִשְׂרָאֵל וְהַזְּמַנִּים.

Baruch atah Adonai, Eloheinu melech ha'olam, asher bachar banu mikol'am, v'rom'manu mikol-lashon, v'kid'shanu b'mitzvotav, vatiten-lanu Adonai Eloheinu b'ahavah moadim l'simchah, chagim uz'manim l'sason et-yom chag hamatzot hazeh. Z'man cheiruteinu, mikra kodesh, zeicher litziat mitzrayim. Ki vanu vacharta v'otanu kidashta mikol ha'amim. umo'adei kod'shecha b'simchah uv'sason hinchaltanu. Baruch atah Adonai, m'kadeish Yisrael v'hazmanim.

Praised are you, Lord our God, Ruler of the universe, Who has chosen us from among the nations, and made us holy with Your mitzvot, and in love given us festivals for joy, and special times for celebration, this Passover, this holy gathering to recall the Exodus from Egypt. You have chosen us, You have shared Your holiness with us among all the nations. For with festive revelations of Your holiness, happiness and joy You have granted us joyfully the holidays. Praised are you, Adonai, Who sanctifies, Israel and the festivals.

Read the following on the **First night** only:

בָּרוּךְ אַתָּה יי אלוהינו מֶלֶךְ הָעוֹלָם, שֶׁהֶחֱיָנוּ וְקִיְּמָנוּ וְהִגִּיעָנוּ לַזְּמַן הַזֶּה.

Baruch atah Adonai, Eloheinu melech ha-olam, she'hecheyanu v'ki'manu v'higi-anu laz'man hazeh.

Praised are you, Adonai, Lord our God, Ruler of the universe, who has given us life, sustained us, and brought us to this season.

Now sit, and lean to the left as you drink the first cup of wine.

Urchatz

The first ritual handwashing prepares us for eating finger foods, *Karpas*, the *hors d'oeuvres* of the Pesach banquet. It sanctifies the act of eating.

Two Volunteers – one to carry the pitcher and the other to pour the water on people's hands.

No blessing is said for this handwashing.

Why Wash Hands Before Karpas?

Why not say a Bracha? Jewish law requires the ritual washing of the hands before eating bread. This washing is accompanied by a blessing. But why do we wash before eating the green vegetables and why in this case is no blessing recited?

During the Passover seder, it is customary to perform a ritual hand-washing before eating the Karpas (green vegetables). This ritual is based on the idea that physical cleanliness is connected to spiritual purity, and it serves as a reminder of the importance of ritual purity in Jewish tradition. In general, it is required to recite a blessing before performing ritual hand-washing in Judaism, but during the seder, this blessing is <u>not</u> recited in order to emphasize that this ritual is only a pious custom and not a requirement. The hand-washing before Karpas is meant to create a sense of sacredness and devotion during the seder, and it is a way of symbolically preparing oneself for this special occasion.

9

Karpas

The First Dipping

Now, take your vegetable and dip it three times in the salt water. Before eating, we recite together:

בָּרוּךְ אַתָּה יי אלוֹהינוּ מֶלֶךְ הָעוֹלָם, בּוֹרֵא פְּרִי הָאֲדָמָה.

Baruch Atah Adonai, Eloheinu Melech ha-olam, borei p'ree ha-adama.

Blessed are you, God, Ruler of Everything, who creates the fruits of the earth.

A Menu of Meanings: Why Karpas?

Karpas is a green vegetable (such as parsley, lettuce, or celery) that is traditionally used during the Passover seder as a symbol of spring and new life. During the seder, a small piece of Karpas is dipped into salt water and eaten as one of the seder's 15 steps or rituals.

The dipping of the Karpas in salt water is meant to symbolize the tears and suffering of the Jewish people during their time in slavery in Egypt. It is also a reminder of the bitterness and hardship that can be present in life. The Karpas ritual is followed by the hand-washing before eating the Matzah, which is another important ritual during the Passover seder. The Matzah is a type of unleavened bread that is symbolic of the hurried flight of the Israelites from Egypt, and it is also a reminder of the simplicity and humility of the Jewish people. Together, the Karpas and the Matzah rituals help to tell the story of the Passover and the liberation of the Israelites from slavery.

Yachatz

Breaking the Matzah

1. **Breaking the Matzah** is one of many ritual acts that turn the food of the Seder into a symbol of meaning.
2. **Count off** the matzot from top to bottom: 1, 2, 3.
    a. The Top matzah is for the usual blessing over bread (**motzi**)
    b. The bottom matzah is for the Hillel sandwich (**Korech**) made with matzah, maror and charoset
3. **Break the middle matzah** in two – it serves a dual role:
    a. The **bigger** portion is to be hidden for the **"afikoman"** and eaten when retrieved from the children for dessert. *It will be the last taste of food at the Seder.*
    b. The **smaller** portion will be eaten with the top matzah when we say the special blessing over matzah at the beginning of the meal.
4. Hide the **afikoman** now.

During the Passover seder, the Yachatz ritual involves breaking the middle Matzah (unleavened bread) on the seder plate in half. One half is set aside to be used later as the Afikoman (a piece of Matzah that is hidden and later found). The other half is returned to the seder plate and is later used in the Hillel sandwich (a sandwich made with Matzah and maror, the bitter herbs).

The breaking of the Matzah during the Yachatz ritual is a reminder of the hurried flight of the Israelites from Egypt and the fact that they did not have time to let their bread rise. It is also a reminder of the simplicity and humility of the Jewish people. The Matzah is symbolic of the bread that the Israelites ate during their time in slavery in Egypt, and breaking it serves as a way of recalling the deprivation and hardship that they experienced during this time.

The Yachatz ritual is an opportunity for the participants in the seder to reflect on the Passover story and the themes of liberation and freedom that it represents. It is also a reminder to be grateful for what we have and to not take our freedom and abundance for granted. Breaking the Matzah is meant to jar us out of our sense of complacency and to help us think about how we can be more kind and understanding towards people who are struggling.

Maggid

Telling the Story

The heart of the Seder is the "maggid" from the term "Haggadah," meaning "storytelling." The storytelling can be flexible and inventive, as this is the longest part of the Seder, <u>it should also be the most creative</u>. That is to say – do not only do what is in the Haggadah, make much of this part up. This Haggadah has a few of the key parts, but Maggid relies on you to make it whole.

Raise the tray with the matzot and say:

Ha lachma anya	הָא לַחְמָא עַנְיָא
Dee achalu avhatana	דִּי אֲכָלוּ אַבְהָתָנָא
B'ara d'meetzrayeem.	בְּאַרְעָא דְמִצְרָיִם.
Kol deechfeen yeitei v'yeichol,	כָּל דִּכְפִין יֵיתֵי וְיֵיכֹל,
Kol deetzreech yeitei v'yeefsach.	כָּל דִּצְרִיךְ יֵיתֵי וְיִפְסַח.
Hashata hacha,	הָשַׁתָּא הָכָא,
L'shanah haba-ah	לְשָׁנָה הַבָּאָה
B'ara d'yisra-el.	בְּאַרְעָא דְיִשְׂרָאֵל.
Hashata avdei,	הָשַׁתָּא עַבְדֵי,
L'shanah haba-ah	לְשָׁנָה הַבָּאָה
B'nei choreen.	בְּנֵי חוֹרִין

This is the bread of affliction, which our ancestors ate in the land of Egypt. Let all who are hungry come and eat. Let all who are in need, come and share the Pesach meal. This year, we are here. Next year, in the land of Israel. This year, we are slaves. Next year, we will be free.

Ha Lachma Anya, which means "This is the bread of poverty," is a passage recited at the beginning of the Passover seder. It is written in Aramaic, a language spoken by Jews in ancient times and used as a common language in the Middle East during the time of the Talmud. Ha Lachma Anya is written in Aramaic because it was the common language of the Jews during the time of the Talmud and because using a foreign language emphasizes the Jews' sense of alienation and strangeness during their time in exile. It also serves as a reminder of the poverty and hardship they experienced. Ha Lachma Anya connects the Passover seder to the Jewish people's rich history and traditions and brings to life the seder's themes and lessons.

(During this time, you may begin refilling the wine cups, but don't drink yet.)

Four Questions

מַה נִּשְׁתַּנָה

Pour the second cup for everyone.
Let the younger children sing "Ma Nishtana."

Why is this night of Passover different from all other nights of the year?	Mah nish-ta-na ha-lai-lah ha-zeh mikol ha-lei-lot?	מַה נִּשְׁתַּנָה הַלַּיְלָה הַזֶּה מִכָּל הַלֵּילוֹת?
On all other nights, we eat either leavened bread or matzahh, why on this night do we eat only **matzahh**?	She-b'chol ha-lei-lot anu och'lin cha-meitz u-matzahh. Ha-laylah hazeh kulo matzahh.	שֶׁבְּכָל הַלֵּילוֹת אָנוּ אוֹכְלִין חָמֵץ וּמַצָּה, הַלַּיְלָה הַזֶּה - כֻּלּוֹ מַצָּה.
On all other nights, we eat vegetables of all kinds, why on this night must we eat bitter herbs (**maror**)?	Sheb'chol ha-lei-lot anu och'lin sh'ar y'rakot. Ha-lai-lah h-azeh maror.	שֶׁבְּכָל הַלֵּילוֹת. אָנוּ אוֹכְלִין שְׁאָר יְרָקוֹת, הַלַּיְלָה הַזֶּה מָרוֹר.
On all other nights, we need not dip Our vegetables even once, But on this night we **dip** twice.	Sheb'chol ha-lei-lot ein anu mat-beelin afee-lu pa-am echat.Ha-lai-lah hazeh sh'tei p'ameem.	שֶׁבְּכָל הַלֵּילוֹת. אֵין אָנוּ מַטְבִּילִין אֲפִילוּ פַּעַם אֶחָת הַלַּיְלָה הַזֶּה שְׁתֵּי פְעָמִים
On all other nights, we eat either sitting upright or reclining, but on this night we all **recline**.	Sheb'khol ha-lei-lot anu och-leem bein yo-shveen u-vein m'su-been, ha-lailah hazeh kulanu m'subeen.	שֶׁבְּכָל הַלֵּילוֹת אָנוּ אוֹכְלִין בֵּין יוֹשְׁבִין וּבֵין מְסֻבִּין הַלַּיְלָה הַזֶּה כֻּלָּנוּ מְסֻבִּין.

Storytelling: Multiple Options

It is now recommended that you take a pause from the Haggadah — and retell the Passover story in some creative ways. Children can do skits for the family, adults can relate the story, or, as we have had ample fun within our family, we do a Passover quiz through Kahoot which is fun and educational (the quiz is public on the Kahoot site and feel free to use it "Passover – Magid Quiz").

Other options – will require a one-month plan to make interactive but worth it:
- Passover Jeopardy: https://www.playfactile.com/search?game=passover
- Passover Games: https://www.baamboozle.com/

The below passage is the most basic traditional passage of the Maggid that will be read to bridge traditions through generations.

עֲבָדִים הָיִינוּ

עֲבָדִים הָיִינוּ לְפַרְעֹה בְּמִצְרָיִם, וַיּוֹצִיאֵנוּ יי אֱלֹהֵינוּ מִשָּׁם בְּיָד חֲזָקָה וּבִזְרוֹעַ נְטוּיָה.

וְאִלּוּ לֹא הוֹצִיא הַקָּדוֹשׁ בָּרוּךְ הוּא אֶת אֲבוֹתֵינוּ מִמִּצְרַיִם, הֲרֵי אָנוּ וּבָנֵינוּ וּבְנֵי בָנֵינוּ מְשֻׁעְבָּדִים הָיִינוּ לְפַרְעֹה בְּמִצְרָיִם.

וַאֲפִילוּ כֻּלָּנוּ חֲכָמִים, כֻּלָּנוּ נְבוֹנִים, כֻּלָּנוּ זְקֵנִים, כֻּלָּנוּ יוֹדְעִים אֶת הַתּוֹרָה, מִצְוָה עָלֵינוּ לְסַפֵּר בִּיצִיאַת מִצְרָיִם.

וְכָל הַמַּרְבֶּה לְסַפֵּר בִּיצִיאַת מִצְרַיִם הֲרֵי זֶה מְשֻׁבָּח.

Avadim hayinu l'faroh b'mitzrayim. Vayotzi-einu Adonai Eloheinu misham, b'yad chazakah uvizroa n'tuyah. V'ilu lo hotzi hakadosh Baruch hu et avoteinu mimitzrayim, harei anu uvaneinu uv'nei vaneinu, m'shubadim hayinu l'faroh b'mitzrayim. Va-afilu kulanu chachamim, kulanu n'vonim, kulanu z'keinim, kulanu yod'im et hatorah, mitzvah aleinu l'sapeir bitzi-at mitzrayim. V'chol hamarbeh l'sapeir bitzi-at mitzrayim, harei zeh m'shubach.

When, in time to come, your children ask you: "What is the meaning of the decrees, laws, and rules that Adonai our God has enjoined upon you?" You shall say to your children: **"We were slaves to Pharoah in Egypt and Adonai freed us from Egypt with a mighty hand and an outstretched arm.** Adonai produced before our eyes great and awful signs and wonders in Egypt, against Pharoah and all his household; and God freed us from there, so that God could take us and give us the land that had been promised on oath to our ancestors."

If God had not taken our ancestors out of Egypt, then we would still be enslaved to Pharaoh in Egypt, along with our children, and our children's children.

Even if all of us were wise, all of us discerning, all of us veteran scholars, and all of us knowledgeable in Torah, it would still be a mitzvah for us to retell the story of the Exodus from Egypt.
So, the more and the longer one expands and embellishes the story, the more commendable it is.

Supplementary Reading below – this does <u>not</u> necessarily have to be read out loud for the Seder. Many like to incorporate it.

Seder of our Sages: Telling of the Story

מַעֲשֶׂה בְּרַבִּי אֱלִיעֶזֶר וְרַבִּי יְהוֹשֻׁעַ וְרַבִּי אֶלְעָזָר בֶּן עֲזַרְיָה וְרַבִּי עֲקִיבָא וְרַבִּי
טַרְפוֹן שֶׁהָיוּ מְסֻבִּין בִּבְנֵי בְרַק, וְהָיוּ מְסַפְּרִים בִּיצִיאַת מִצְרַיִם כָּל אוֹתוֹ הַלַּיְלָה
עַד שֶׁבָּאוּ תַלְמִידֵיהֶם וְאָמְרוּ לָהֶם: רַבּוֹתֵינוּ, הִגִּיעַ זְמַן קְרִיאַת שְׁמַע שֶׁל
שַׁחֲרִית.

Ma-aseh b'rabi Eli-ezer, v'rabi Y'hoshua, v'rabi Elazar ben azaryah, v'rabi Akiva, v'rabi Tarfon, she-hayu m'subin bivnei vrak, v'hayu m'sap'rim bitzi-at mitzrayim, kol oto halaylah, ad sheba-u talmideihem v'am'ru lahem. Raboteinu, higi-a z'man k'ri-at sh'ma, shel shacharit.

It once happened that Rabbis Eliezer, Joshua, Elazar ben Azaryah, Akiva and Tarfon were reclining at the Seder table in Bnei Brak. They spent the whole night discussing the Exodus until their students came and said to them: "Rabbis, it is time for us to recite the Shema

אָמַר אֶלְעָזָר בֶּן עֲזַרְיָה : הֲרֵי אֲנִי כְּבֶן שִׁבְעִים שָׁנָה, וְלֹא זָכִיתִי שֶׁתֵּאָמֵר יְצִיאַת
מִצְרַיִם בַּלֵּילוֹת עַד שֶׁדְּרָשָׁהּ בֶּן זוֹמָא: שֶׁנֶּאֱמַר, לְמַעַן תִּזְכֹּר אֶת יוֹם צֵאתְךָ
מֵאֶרֶץ מִצְרַיִם כָּל יְמֵי חַיֶּיךָ יְמֵי חַיֶּיךָ הַיָּמִים, כָּל יְמֵי חַיֶּיךָ - הַלֵּילוֹת. וַחֲכָמִים
אוֹמְרִים: יְמֵי חַיֶּיךָ הָעוֹלָם הַזֶּה, כָּל יְמֵי חַיֶּיךָ לְהָבִיא לִימוֹת הַמָּשִׁיחַ

Amar rabi Elazar ben Azaryah. Harei ani k'ven shivim shanah, v'lo zachiti, shetei-ameir y'tzi-at mitzrayim baleilot. Ad shed'rashah ben zoma. Shene-emar: l'ma-an tizkor, et yom tzeitcha mei-eretz mitzrayim, kol y'mei chayecha. Y'mei chayecha hayamim. Kol y'mei chayecha haleilot. Vachachamim om'rim. Y'mei chayecha ha-olam hazeh. Kol y'mei chayecha l'havi limot hamashi-ach.

Rabbi Elazar ben Azaryah said: "I am like a seventy-year old man and I have not succeeded in understanding why the Exodus from Egypt should be mentioned at night, until Ben Zoma explained it by quoting: "In order that you may remember the day you left Egypt all the days of your life." The Torah adds the word all to the phrase the days of your life to indicate that the nights are meant as well. The sages declare that "the days of your life" means the present world and "all " includes the messianic era.

A Passover Skit

Not required, but as an idea that can be used during the Maggid section – the main point being – BE CREATIVE! – make Maggid a family experience, not simply recitation.

Child 1 is playing the part of an Israelite Slave
Child 2 is playing the part of Pharaoh

Slave: (sitting on the ground, looking sad) Oh, I'm so tired from all this hard work. I wish we could be free from slavery.

Pharoah: (standing tall, dressed in a Pharaoh costume) Ha! You'll never be free! You are my slaves and you will work for me forever!.

Slave: (stands up) But God is on our side. He will help us escape from this slavery.

Pharoah: (laughs) What can one God do against the mighty Pharaoh?

Slave: (takes out a book and begins reading)
"And God sent ten plagues upon Pharaoh and the Egyptians. The first plague was the Nile turning to blood. The second plague was the frogs. The third plague was the lice. The fourth plague was the wild animals. The fifth plague was the pestilence on the livestock. The sixth plague was the boils. The seventh plague was the hail. The eighth plague was the locusts. The ninth plague was the darkness. The tenth plague was the death of the firstborn."

Pharoah: (gasps) This is terrible! I must let the Israelites go!

Slave: (smiling) And that's exactly what Pharaoh did. The Israelites were finally free from slavery and they celebrated with the first Passover Seder.

Pharoah: (bowing) I am sorry for treating you so poorly. I will never enslave anyone again.

Slave: (smiling) Thank you, Pharaoh. We are grateful to be free and to celebrate the Passover Seder each year to remember our liberation.
(Both children bow to each other and the skit ends)

The Four Children

The story of the Four Children is meant to illustrate the different ways that people approach the Passover seder and the lessons of the Passover story.

According to the Haggadah, there are four types of children: the **wise** child, the **wicked** child, the **simple** child, and the child who **does not know how** to ask. Each of these children represents a different approach to the Passover seder and the lessons that it teaches.

The wise child asks questions and seeks to understand the meaning of the Passover story. The wicked child is rebellious and does not want to participate in the seder. The simple child is sincere and wants to know more about the Passover story, but does not know how to ask. The child who does not know how to ask represents those who are not present at the seder or who do not have the opportunity to learn about the Passover story.

Overall, the story of the Four Children is meant to encourage participation in the Passover seder and to encourage people to think about the meaning and significance of the Passover story. It is a way of reminding us that the Passover seder is a time for learning and reflection, and that there is something to be gained from the seder experience for people of all ages and backgrounds.

בָּרוּךְ הַמָּקוֹם, בָּרוּךְ הוּא. בָּרוּךְ שֶׁנָּתַן תּוֹרָה לְעַמּוֹ יִשְׂרָאֵל, בָּרוּךְ הוּא.

Blessed be God, Blessed be that One, Blessed be the Giver of the Torah to the people Israel, Blessed be that One.

כְּנֶגֶד אַרְבָּעָה בָנִים דִּבְּרָה תּוֹרָה . אֶחָד חָכָם, וְאֶחָד רָשָׁע, וְאֶחָד תָּם, וְאֶחָד שֶׁאֵינוֹ יוֹדֵעַ לִשְׁאוֹל.

Baruch hamakom, baruch hu. Baruch shenatan torah l'amo yisra-eil, baruch hu.
K'neged arba-ah vanim dib'rah torah. Echad chacham, v'echad rasha, v'echad tam,
v'echad she-eino yodei-a lishol

The Torah speaks of four types of children: one is wise, one is wicked, one is simple, and
one does not know how to ask.

חָכָם מָה הוּא אוֹמֵר? מָה הָעֵדוֹת וְהַחֻקִּים וְהַמִּשְׁפָּטִים אֲשֶׁר צִוָּה יי אֱלֹהֵינוּ אֶתְכֶם? וְאַף אַתָּה
אֱמָר לוֹ כְּהִלְכוֹת הַפֶּסַח: אֵין מַפְטִירִין אַחַר הַפֶּסַח אֲפִיקוֹמָן.

Chacham mah hu omeir? Mah ha-eidot v'hachukim v'hamishpatim, asher tzivah
Adonai Eloheinu etchem? V'af atah emor lo k'hilchot hapesach. Ein maftirin achar
hapesach afikoman.

The Wise One asks: "What is the meaning of the laws and traditions God has
commanded?" (Deuteronomy 6:20) You should teach him all the traditions of Passover, even to
the last detail.

רָשָׁע מָה הוּא אוֹמֵר? מָה הָעֲבֹדָה הַזֹּאת לָכֶם? לָכֶם - וְלֹא לוֹ. וּלְפִי שֶׁהוֹצִיא אֶת עַצְמוֹ מִן
הַכְּלָל כָּפַר בְּעִקָּר. וְאַף אַתָּה הַקְהֵה אֶת שִׁנָּיו וֶאֱמָר לוֹ: בַּעֲבוּר זֶה עָשָׂה יי לִי בְּצֵאתִי
מִמִּצְרָיִם. לִי - וְלֹא לוֹ. אִילוּ הָיָה שָׁם, לֹא הָיָה נִגְאָל.

Rasha, mah hu omer? Mah ha-avodah ha-zot lachem? Lachem v'lo lo. Ul'fi shehotzi
et atzmo min hak'lal, kafar ba-ikar. V'af atah hakheih et shinav, ve-emor lo. Ba-avur
zeh, asah Adonai li, b'tzeiti mimitzrayim, li v'lo lo. Ilu hayah sham, lo hayah nigal.

The Wicked One asks: "What does this ritual mean to you?" (Exodus 12:26) By using the
expression "to you" he excludes himself from his people and denies God. Shake his
arrogance and say to him: "It is because of what the Lord did for me when I came out of
Egypt..." (Exodus 13:8) "For me" and not for him -- for had he been in Egypt, he would not
have been freed.

תָּם מָה הוּא אוֹמֵר? מַה זֹּאת? וְאָמַרְתָּ אֵלָיו: בְּחֹזֶק יָד הוֹצִיאָנוּ יי מִמִּצְרָיִם, מִבֵּית עֲבָדִים.

Tam mah hu omeir? Mah zot? V'amarta eilav. B'chozek yad hotzi-anu Adonai
mimitzrayim mibeit avadim.

The Simple One asks: "What is all this?" You should tell him: "It was with a mighty hand
that the Lord took us out of Egypt, out of the house of bondage."

וְשֶׁאֵינוֹ יוֹדֵעַ לִשְׁאוֹל - אַתְּ פְּתַח לוֹ, שֶׁנֶּאֱמַר: וְהִגַּדְתָּ לְבִנְךָ בַּיּוֹם הַהוּא לֵאמֹר, בַּעֲבוּר זֶה
עָשָׂה יי לִי בְּצֵאתִי מִמִּצְרָיִם.

V'she-eino yodei-a lishol, at p'tach lo. Shene-emar. V'higadta l'vincha, bayom hahu leimor. Ba-avur zeh asah Adonai li, b'tzeiti mimitzrayim.

As for the One Who Does Not Know How To Ask, you should open the discussion for him, as it is written: "And you shall explain to your child on that day, 'It is because of what the Lord did for me when I came out of Egypt." (Exodus 13:8)

Standing Up for Us

Cover the matzah, raise your cup and sing together, acknowledging God's commitment to our survival. Afterwards, set your cup down and uncover the matzah for the continuation of Maggid.

וְהִיא שֶׁעָמְדָה לַאֲבוֹתֵינוּ וְלָנוּ וְהִיא שֶׁעָמְדָה, וְהִיא שֶׁעָמְדָה לַאֲבוֹתֵינוּ וְלָנוּ. שֶׁלֹּא אֶחָד בִּלְבַד עָמַד עָלֵינוּ לְכַלּוֹתֵנוּ שֶׁלֹּא אֶחָד בִּלְבַד עָמַד עָלֵינוּ לְכַלּוֹתֵנוּ. אֶלָּא שֶׁבְּכָל דּוֹר וָדוֹר עוֹמְדִים עָלֵינוּ לְכַלּוֹתֵנוּ אֶלָּא שֶׁבְּכָל דּוֹר וָדוֹר עוֹמְדִים עָלֵינוּ לְכַלּוֹתֵנוּ. וְהַקָּדוֹשׁ בָּרוּךְ הוּא מַצִּילֵנוּ מִיָּדָם וְהַקָּדוֹשׁ בָּרוּךְ הוּא מַצִּילֵנוּ מִיָּדָם.

Ve-hi she-am-dah la-a-vo-tei-nu ve-la-nu ve-he-lo e-chad bil-vad a-mad a-lei-nu le-cha-loi-sei-nu. E-lah she-be-chal dor va-dor om-dim a-lei-nu le-cha-loi-sei-nu ve-Ha-ka-dosh Ba-ruch Hu ma-tzi-lei-nu mi-ya-dam.

And this has stood by our fathers and us, for not just one rose against us to annihilate us, but in every generation there are those who rise to annihilate us. And the Holy One Blessed is He saves us from their hands.

'Arami Oved Avi'

The Wandering Jew

On Pesach each of us retells our story of wandering and homecoming, as did the farmer bringing the first fruits to Jerusalem.

אֲרַמִּי אֹבֵד אָבִי וַיֵּרֶד מִצְרַיְמָה וַיָּגָר שָׁם בִּמְתֵי מְעָט וַיְהִי שָׁם לְגוֹי גָּדוֹל עָצוּם וָרָב: וַיָּרֵעוּ אֹתָנוּ הַמִּצְרִים וַיְעַנּוּנוּ וַיִּתְּנוּ עָלֵינוּ עֲבֹדָה קָשָׁה: וַנִּצְעַק אֶל יְהֹוָה אֱלֹהֵי אֲבֹתֵינוּ וַיִּשְׁמַע יְהֹוָה אֶת קֹלֵנוּ וַיַּרְא אֶת עָנְיֵנוּ וְאֶת עֲמָלֵנוּ וְאֶת לַחֲצֵנוּ: וַיּוֹצִאֵנוּ יְהֹוָה מִמִּצְרַיִם בְּיָד חֲזָקָה וּבִזְרֹעַ נְטוּיָה וּבְמֹרָא גָּדֹל וּבְאֹתוֹת וּבְמֹפְתִים: וַיְבִאֵנוּ אֶל הַמָּקוֹם הַזֶּה וַיִּתֶּן לָנוּ אֶת הָאָרֶץ הַזֹּאת אֶרֶץ זָבַת חָלָב וּדְבָשׁ: וְעַתָּה הִנֵּה הֵבֵאתִי אֶת רֵאשִׁית פְּרִי הָאֲדָמָה אֲשֶׁר נָתַתָּה לִּי יְהֹוָה.

"My Ancestor was a wandering Aramean. He descended to Egypt and resided there in small number. He became a nation – great, powerful and numerous. The Egyptians treated us badly. They persecuted us and put us under hard labor. We cried out to Adonai, the God of our ancestors. God heard our voice. God saw our persecution, our toil and our oppression. God took us out of Egypt with a strong hand and an outstretched arm, with awesome power, signs and wonders. God brought us to this place and gave us this land, a land of milk and honey. Now I have brought the first fruits of this soil, which you, God, gave me." (Deut. 26:1-10)

The Ten Plagues

אֵלּוּ עֶשֶׂר מַכּוֹת שֶׁהֵבִיא הַקָּדוֹשׁ בָּרוּךְ הוּא עַל הַמִּצְרִים בְּמִצְרַיִם , וְאֵלּוּ הֵן.

Eilu eser makot sheheivi hakadosh baruch hu al hamitzrim b'mitzrayim, v'eilu hein:
These are the ten Plagues that the Holy One brought upon Egypt.

At the mention of each plague, remove a drop from your cup.

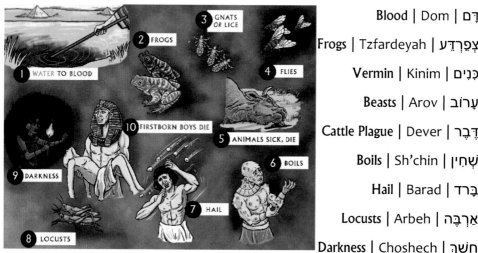

Blood | Dom | דָּם

Frogs | Tzfardeyah | צְפַרְדֵּעַ

Vermin | Kinim | כִּנִּים

Beasts | Arov | עָרוֹב

Cattle Plague | Dever | דֶּבֶר

Boils | Sh'chin | שְׁחִין

Hail | Barad | בָּרָד

Locusts | Arbeh | אַרְבֶּה

Darkness | Choshech | חֹשֶׁךְ

Slaying of First Born | Makat Bechorot | מַכַּת בְּכוֹרוֹת

Since ancient versions varied as to the nature and number of the plagues, it is believed that Rabbi Jehudah instituted these three phrases or acronyms to confirm the version in Exodus. Accordingly we now remove another three drops of wine from our cup of joy.

רַבִּי יְהוּדָה הָיָה נוֹתֵן בָּהֶם סִמָּנִים:
Rabi Y'hudah hayah notein bahem simanim.
Rabbi Yehuda would assign the plagues three mnenomic signs:
דְּצַ"ךְ עַדַ"שׁ בְּאַחַ"ב.
D'TZ"KH A-Da"SH B'AH"

21

THE TEN PLAGUES

(Please Color Me)

Dayeinu

'It would have been enough'

Dayeinu commemorates a long list of miraculous things God did for us, any one of which would have been pretty amazing just by itself. The word "dayeinu" means "it would have been enough" in Hebrew, and the song is structured around a series of verses that begin with this phrase. Each verse enumerates a different blessing or miracle that God performed for the Israelites and declares that if God had only done this one thing, it would have been enough for us.

The purpose of Dayeinu is to express gratitude to God for the many blessings and miracles that God has bestowed upon the Jewish people. It is a way of reminding us of all that God has done for us and of the many ways in which God has helped us and guided us throughout history. Dayeinu is an important part of the Passover seder and is a way of bringing to life the themes of liberation and gratitude that are central to the seder experience.

Five Stanzas of <u>Leaving Slavery</u>

1) If He had brought us out of Egypt.
2) If He had executed justice upon the Egyptians.
3) If He had executed justice upon their gods.
4) If He had slain their first-born.
5) If He had given us their health and wealth.

כַּמָה מַעֲלוֹת טוֹבוֹת לַמָקוֹם עָלֵינוּ.

אִלוּ הוֹצִיאָנוּ מִמִּצְרַיִם, וְלֹא עָשָׂה בָהֶם שְׁפָטִים, דַּיֵּנוּ.
אִלוּ עָשָׂה בָהֶם שְׁפָטִים, וְלֹא עָשָׂה בֵאלֹהֵיהֶם, דַּיֵּנוּ.
אִלוּ עָשָׂה בֵאלֹהֵיהֶם, וְלֹא הָרַג אֶת בְּכוֹרֵיהֶם, דַּיֵּנוּ.
אִלוּ הָרַג אֶת בְּכוֹרֵיהֶם, וְלֹא נָתַן לָנוּ אֶת מָמוֹנָם, דַּיֵּנוּ.
אִלוּ נָתַן לָנוּ אֶת מָמוֹנָם, וְלֹא קָרַע לָנוּ אֶת הַיָּם, דַּיֵּנוּ.

Five Stanzas of <u>Miracles</u>

6) If He had split the sea for us.
7) If He had led us through on dry land.
8) If He had drowned our oppressors.
9) If He had provided for our needs in the wilderness for 40 years.
10) If He had fed us manna.

אִלוּ קָרַע לָנוּ אֶת הַיָּם, וְלֹא הֶעֱבִירָנוּ בְּתוֹכוֹ בֶּחָרָבָה, דַּיֵּנוּ.
אִלוּ הֶעֱבִירָנוּ בְּתוֹכוֹ בֶּחָרָבָה, וְלֹא שָׁקַע צָרֵנוּ בְּתוֹכוֹ, דַּיֵּנוּ.
אִלוּ שָׁקַע צָרֵנוּ בְּתוֹכוֹ, וְלֹא סִפֵּק צָרְכֵּנוּ בַּמִּדְבָּר אַרְבָּעִים שָׁנָה, דַּיֵּנוּ.
אִלוּ סִפֵּק צָרְכֵּנוּ בַּמִּדְבָּר אַרְבָּעִים שָׁנָה, וְלֹא הֶאֱכִילָנוּ אֶת הַמָּן, דַּיֵּנוּ.
אִלוּ הֶאֱכִילָנוּ אֶת הַמָּן, וְלֹא נָתַן לָנוּ אֶת הַשַּׁבָּת, דַּיֵּנוּ.

Five Stanzas of <u>Being With God</u>

11) If He had given us Shabbat.
12) If He had led us to Mount Sinai.
13) If He had given us the Torah.
14) If He had brought us into the Land of Israel.
15) If He built the Temple for us.

אִלוּ נָתַן לָנוּ אֶת הַשַּׁבָּת, וְלֹא קֵרְבָנוּ לִפְנֵי הַר סִינַי, דַּיֵּנוּ.
אִלוּ קֵרְבָנוּ לִפְנֵי הַר סִינַי, וְלֹא נָתַן לָנוּ אֶת הַתּוֹרָה, דַּיֵּנוּ.
אִלוּ נָתַן לָנוּ אֶת הַתּוֹרָה, וְלֹא הִכְנִיסָנוּ לְאֶרֶץ יִשְׂרָאֵל, דַּיֵּנוּ.
אִלוּ הִכְנִיסָנוּ לְאֶרֶץ יִשְׂרָאֵל, וְלֹא בָנָה לָנוּ אֶת בֵּית הַבְּחִירָה, דַּיֵּנוּ.

Pesach, Matzah and Maror

Obligations of the Holiday

The Maggid Section (devoted to storytelling and explanations) is almost complete. Before eating the Seder's edible symbols, according to the Haggadah, Rabban Gamliel identified three essential foods that are to be included in the Passover seder:

(1) **Maror** captures the bitterness of the enslavement;
(2) The **Pesach Lamb**, The Passover sacrifice, which was a lamb or kid goat that was slaughtered and roasted in accordance with the commandments of the Torah;
(3) **Matzah** stands for the following morning, when Israel was rushed out of Egypt with no time to let their dough rise.

These three essential foods are known as the "korban Pesach," or the Passover sacrifice, and they are central to the Passover seder. They are symbolic of the liberation of the Israelites from slavery in Egypt and are a way of remembering the events of the Passover story in a tangible and meaningful way.

רַבָּן גַּמְלִיאֵל הָיָה אוֹמֵר:כָּל שֶׁלֹּא אָמַר שְׁלֹשָׁה דְבָרִים אֵלּוּ בַּפֶּסַח, לֹא יָצָא יְדֵי חוֹבָתוֹ, וְאֵלּוּ הֵן: פֶּסַח, מַצָּה, וּמָרוֹר.

Rabban Gamlieil hayah omeir: kol shelo amar sh'loshah d'varim eilu bapesach, lo yatza y'dei chovato, v'eilu hein: Pesach, Matzahh, Umaror..

"Rabbi Gamliel used to say: "All who have not explained the significance of three things during the Pesach Seder have not yet fulfilled their duty. The three are: the **Pesach lamb**, the **matzah** and the **maror**."

(Leader asks the question in the following three and everyone answers) While pointing (but do not rasie) to the shank bone:

פֶּסַח שֶׁהָיוּ אֲבוֹתֵינוּ אוֹכְלִים בִּזְמַן שֶׁבֵּית הַמִּקְדָּשׁ הָיָה קַיָּם, עַל שׁוּם מָה? עַל שׁוּם שֶׁפָּסַח הַקָּדוֹשׁ בָּרוּךְ הוּא עַל בָּתֵּי אֲבוֹתֵינוּ בְמִצְרַיִם , שֶׁנֶּאֱמַר: וַאֲמַרְתֶּם זֶבַח פֶּסַח הוּא לַיי, אֲשֶׁר פָּסַח עַל בָּתֵּי בְנֵי יִשְׂרָאֵל בְּמִצְרַיִם בְּנָגְפּוֹ אֶת מִצְרַיִם , וְאֶת בָּתֵּינוּ הִצִּיל? וַיִּקֹּד הָעָם וַיִּשְׁתַּחֲווּ.

Pesach shehayu avoteinu och'lim, bizman shebeit hamikdash hayah kayam, al shum mah? Al shum shepasach hakadosh baruch hu al batei avoteinu b'mitzrayim, shene'emar: va'amartem zevach pesach hu l'Adonai, asher pasach al batei v'nei Yisrael b'mitzrayim, b'nagpo et mitzrayim v'et bateinu hitzil, vayikod ha'am vayishtachavu.

"Pesach Al Shum Ma?" – The Passover lamb (that our ancestors ate in the days of the Temple) – why did we used to eat it?

To Remind ourselves that God **passed over** our ancestors' houses in Egypt (at this very hour on this very date). Moshe has already instructed us: "When your children ask you, 'What do you mean by this ceremony?' you shall say: 'It is the Passover offering to Adonai, because God **passed over** the houses of Israel in Egypt when God struck the Egyptians, but saver our houses.'"

Everyone holds up matzah:

מַצָּה זוֹ שֶׁאָנוּ אוֹכְלִים, עַל שׁוּם מַה? עַל שׁוּם שֶׁלֹּא הִסְפִּיק בְּצֵקָם שֶׁל אֲבוֹתֵינוּ
לְהַחֲמִיץ עַד שֶׁנִּגְלָה עֲלֵיהֶם מֶלֶךְ מַלְכֵי הַמְּלָכִים, הַקָּדוֹשׁ בָּרוּךְ הוּא, וּגְאָלָם, שֶׁנֶּאֱמַר:
וַיֹּאפוּ אֶת הַבָּצֵק אֲשֶׁר הוֹצִיאוּ מִמִּצְרַיִם עֻגֹת מַצּוֹת, כִּי לֹא חָמֵץ, כִּי גֹרְשׁוּ מִמִּצְרַיִם
וְלֹא יָכְלוּ לְהִתְמַהְמֵהַּ, וְגַם צֵדָה לֹא עָשׂוּ לָהֶם.

Matzahh zeh sheanu och'lim, al shum mah? Al shum shelo hispik b'tzeikam shel avoteinu l'hachamitz ad sheniglah aleihem melech malchei ham'lachim, hakadosh baruch hu, ug'alam, shene'emar: vayofu et habatzeik asher hotziu mimitzrayim ugot matzot, ki lo chameitz, ki gor'shu mimitzrayim v'lo yachlu l'hitmahmeiha, v'gam tzeidah lo asu lahem.

"Matzah Al Shum Ma?" – **This matzah!** Why do we eat it?

To remind ourselves that even before the dough of our ancestors in Egypt had time to rise and become leavened, the King of kings, the Holy One revealed Himself and redeemed them. The Torah says: " *They baked unleavened cakes of dough that they had taken out of Egypt, for it was not leavened, since they had been driven out of Egypt and could not delay; nor had they prepared any provisions for themselves.* "

Everyone raises maror from the Seder plate:

מָרוֹר זֶה שֶׁאָנוּ אוֹכְלִים, עַל שׁוּם מַה? עַל שׁוּם שֶׁמֵּרְרוּ הַמִּצְרִים אֶת חַיֵּי אֲבוֹתֵינוּ
בְּמִצְרַיִם , שֶׁנֶּאֱמַר: וַיְמָרֲרוּ אֶת חַיֵּיהֶם בַּעֲבֹדָה קָשָׁה, בְּחֹמֶר וּבִלְבֵנִים וּבְכָל עֲבֹדָה
בַּשָּׂדֶה אֵת כָּל עֲבֹדָתָם אֲשֶׁר עָבְדוּ בָהֶם בְּפָרֶךְ.

Maror zeh sheanu och'lim, al shum mah? Al shum shemeir'ru hamitzrim et chayei avoteinu b'mitzrayim, shene'emar: vayamararu et chayeihem baavodah kashah, b'chomer uvilveinim uv'chol avodah basadeh et kol avodatam asher avdu vahem b'farech.

"Maror Al Shum Ma?" – **This maror!** Why do we eat it?

To Remind ourselves that the Egyptians embittered our ancestor's lives. " *They embittered their lives with hard labor, with mortar and bricks and with all sorts of field labor. Whatever the task, they worked them ruthlessly.* "

In Every Generation

דֹּור וָדֹור

"The Exodus from Egypt occurs in every human being, in every ear, in every year and even on every day," said Hassidic Rabbi Nachman of Bratslav. At the Seder we must try to empathize with that original liberation and to discover its relevance throughout the generations.

בְּכָל דֹּור וָדֹור חַיָּב אָדָם לִרְאֹות אֶת עַצְמֹו כְאִלּו הוא יָצָא מִמִּצְרַיִם , שֶׁנֶּאֱמַר: וְהִגַּדְתָּ לְבִנְךָ בַּיֹום הַהוא לֵאמֹר, בַּעֲבוּר זֶה עָשָׂה יי לִי בְּצֵאתִי מִמִּצְרַיִם .

לֹא אֶת אֲבֹותֵינו בִּלְבָד גָּאַל הַקָּדֹוש בָּרוּךְ הוא, אֶלָּא אַף אֹותָנו גָּאַל עִמָּהֶם, שֶׁנֶּאֱמַר: וְאֹותָנו הֹוצִיא מִשָּׁם , לְמַעַן הָבִיא אֹתָנו, לָתֶת לָנו אֶת הָאָרֶץ אֲשֶׁר נִשְׁבַּע לַאֲבֹתֵנו.

B'chol dor vador chayav adam lirot et atzmo k'ilu hu yatza mimitzrayim, shene'emar: v'higadta l'vincha bayom hahu leimor, ba'avur zeh asah Adonai li b'tzeiti mimitzrayim.

Lo et avoteinu bilvad ga'al hakadosh baruch hu, ela af otanu ga'al imahem, shene'emar: v'otanu hotzi misham, l'ma'an havi otanu, latet lanu et ha'aretz asher nishba la'avoteinu.

In every generation, one must see himself as if he himself had personally come out of Egypt, as it is said: "You should say to your son on that day, 'It is because of that which God did to me when I left Egypt.'

Not only were our ancestors redeemed by the Holy One, but even we were redeemed with them. Just as it says: "God took us out form there in order to bring us and to give us the land God swore to our ancestors."

Toast for completing Maggid

After the Maggid (telling of the Passover story) has been completed at the Passover seder, it is traditional to make a toast with the third cup of wine. This toast is a way of celebrating the completion of the Maggid and the fact that the Passover story has been told.

The third cup of wine is known as the Cup of Redemption, and it is symbolic of the liberation of the Israelites from slavery in Egypt. By making a toast with this cup, the participants in the seder are expressing their gratitude for the redemption of the Israelites and for the many blessings and miracles that God performed for them.

In addition to symbolizing the redemption of the Israelites, the toast with the third cup of wine is also a way of celebrating the present moment and of coming together as a community to remember and honor the past. It is a time for joy and celebration, and it is a way of bringing to life the themes of liberation and freedom that are central to the Passover seder.

Cover the matzah and raise the cup of wine until it is drunk at the end of Maggid.

לְפִיכָךְ אֲנַחְנוּ חַיָּבִים לְהוֹדוֹת, לְהַלֵּל, לְשַׁבֵּחַ, לְפָאֵר, לְרוֹמֵם, לְהַדֵּר, לְבָרֵךְ, לְעַלֵּה
וּלְקַלֵּס לְמִי שֶׁעָשָׂה לַאֲבוֹתֵינוּ וְלָנוּ אֶת כָּל הַנִּסִּים הָאֵלּוּ: הוֹצִיאָנוּ מֵעַבְדוּת לְחֵרוּת
מִיָּגוֹן לְשִׂמְחָה, וּמֵאֵבֶל לְיוֹם טוֹב, וּמֵאֲפֵלָה לְאוֹר גָּדוֹל, וּמִשִּׁעְבּוּד לִגְאֻלָּה. וְנֹאמַר
לְפָנָיו שִׁירָה חֲדָשָׁה: הַלְלוּיָהּ

L'fichach anachnu chayavim l'hodot, l'hallel, l'shabeiach, l'faeir, l'romeim, l'hadeir, l'vareich, l'aleih ul'kaleis, l'mi she'asah a'avoteinu v'lanu et kol hanisim haeilu: hotzianu meiavdut l'cheirut miyagon l'simchah, umei'eivel l'yom tov, umei'afeilah l'or gadol, umishibud ligulah. V'nomar l'fanav shirah chadashah: halleluyah.

Therefore we owe it to God: to thank, to sing, to praise and honr, to glorify and bless, to raise up and acclaim the One who has done all these wonders for our ancestors and for us.

God took us from **slavery to freedom,**
from **sorrow to joy,**
from **mourning to festivity,**
from **thick darkness to a great light,**
from **enslavement to redemption!**

Let us sing before God, a new song.
HALLELUJAH!

Hallel: Psalm 13

The first part of Hallel (Psalms 113-114) begins here before the meal and the rest is completed after eating.

הַלְלוּיָהּ הַלְלוּ עַבְדֵי יי, הַלְלוּ אֶת שֵׁם יי. יְהִי שֵׁם יי מְבֹרָךְ מֵעַתָּה וְעַד עוֹלָם. מִמִּזְרַח שֶׁמֶשׁ עַד מְבוֹאוֹ מְהֻלָּל שֵׁם יי. רָם עַל כָּל גּוֹיִם יי, עַל הַשָּׁמַיִם כְּבוֹדוֹ. מִי כַּיי אֱלֹהֵינוּ הַמַּגְבִּיהִי לָשָׁבֶת, הַמַּשְׁפִּילִי לִרְאוֹת בַּשָּׁמַיִם וּבָאָרֶץ? מְקִימִי מֵעָפָר דָּל, מֵאַשְׁפֹּת יָרִים אֶבְיוֹן, לְהוֹשִׁיבִי עִם נְדִיבִים, עִם נְדִיבֵי עַמּוֹ. מוֹשִׁיבִי עֲקֶרֶת הַבַּיִת, אֵם הַבָּנִים שְׂמֵחָה. הַלְלוּיָהּ.

Praise the Lord! Praise, you servants of the Lord, praise the name of the Lord. Blessed be the name of the Lord from this time forth and forever. From the rising of the sun to its setting, the Lord's name is to be praised. High above all nations is the Lord; above the heavens is His glory. Who is like the Lord our God, who though enthroned on high, looks down upon heaven and earth? He raises the poor man out of the dust and lifts the needy one out of the trash heap, to seat them with nobles, with the nobles of His people. He turns the barren wife into a happy mother of children. Halleluyah!

בְּצֵאת יִשְׂרָאֵל מִמִּצְרַיִם , בֵּית יַעֲקֹב מֵעַם לֹעֵז, הָיְתָה יְהוּדָה לְקָדְשׁוֹ, יִשְׂרָאֵל מַמְשְׁלוֹתָיו. הַיָּם רָאָה וַיָּנֹס, הַיַּרְדֵּן יִסֹּב לְאָחוֹר. הֶהָרִים רָקְדוּ כְאֵילִים, גְּבָעוֹת - כִּבְנֵי צֹאן. מַה לְּךָ הַיָּם כִּי תָנוּס, הַיַּרְדֵּן - תִּסֹּב לְאָחוֹר, הֶהָרִים - תִּרְקְדוּ כְאֵילִים, גְּבָעוֹת - כִּבְנֵי צֹאן. מִלְּפְנֵי אָדוֹן חוּלִי אָרֶץ, מִלְּפְנֵי אֱלוֹהַ יַעֲקֹב. הַהֹפְכִי הַצּוּר אֲגַם מָיִם, חַלָּמִישׁ - לְמַעְיְנוֹ מָיִם.

When Israel went out of Egypt, When the household of Jacob left a people with a strange tongue, Judah became the place from which God's holiness went forth, Israel became the seat from which the world would know of Gods rule. The sea looked and fled, The Jordan reversed its curse. Mountains skipped like rams and the hills jumped about like young lambs. What is happening that you turn back, O sea, Jordan, why do you reverse your course? Mountains, why do you skip like rams And hills why do you jump like lambs? You are beholding the face of your Creator, Before God, before the God of Jacob, Turning rocks into swirling waters and stone into a flowing spring.

28

2nd Cup

The Second Cup of Wine

We conclude the long Maggid section by drinking the second cup of wine, *the Cup of Redemption*. Recline on a pillow to the left and drink at least half the second cup of wine.

בָּרוּךְ אתה יי אֱלֹהֵינוּ מֶלֶךְ הָעוֹלָם, אֲשֶׁר גְּאָלָנוּ וְגָאַל אֶת אֲבוֹתֵינוּ מִמִּצְרַיִם , וְהִגִּיעָנוּ לַלַּיְלָה הַזֶּה לֶאֱכָל בּוֹ מַצָּה וּמָרוֹר. כֵּן יי אֱלֹהֵינוּ וֵאלֹהֵי אֲבוֹתֵינוּ יַגִּיעֵנוּ לְמוֹעֲדִים וְלִרְגָלִים אֲחֵרִים הַבָּאִים לִקְרָאתֵנוּ לְשָׁלוֹם, שְׂמֵחִים בְּבִנְיַן עִירֶךָ וְשָׂשִׂים בַּעֲבוֹדָתֶךָ. וְנֹאכַל שָׁם מִן הַזְּבָחִים וּמִן הַפְּסָחִים אֲשֶׁר יַגִּיעַ דָּמָם עַל קִיר מִזְבַּחֲךָ לְרָצוֹן, וְנוֹדֶה לְךָ שִׁיר חָדָשׁ עַל גְּאֻלָּתֵנוּ וְעַל פְּדוּת נַפְשֵׁנוּ. בָּרוּךְ אַתָּה יי גָּאַל יִשְׂרָאֵל.

בָּרוּךְ אַתָּה יי אֱלֹהֵינוּ מֶלֶךְ הָעוֹלָם בּוֹרֵא פְּרִי הַגָּפֶן.

Baruch atah Adonai, Eloheinu Melech ha'olam, asher g'alanu v'ga'al et avoteinu mimitzrayim, v'higianu lalaylah hazeh le'echol bo matzahh umaror. Kein Adonai Eloheinu vEilohei avoteinu yagi'einu l'mo'adim v'lirgalim acheirim haba'im likrateinu l'shalom, s'meichim b'vinyan irecha v'sasim ba'avodatecha. V'nochal sham min hazvachim umin hapsachim asher yagia damam al kir mizbachacha l'ratzon, v'nodeh l'cha shir chadash al g'ulateinu v'al p'dut nafsheinu. Baruch Atah Adonai, ga'al Yisrael.
Baruch Atah Adonai, Eloheinu Melech haolam, borei p'ri hagafen.

Praised are you, Adonai, our God, sovereign of the universe, who has redeemed us and our fathers from Egypt and enabled us to reach this night that we may eat matzo and maror. Lord our God and God of our fathers, enable us to reach also the forthcoming holidays and festivals in peace, rejoicing in the rebuilding of Zion your city, and joyful at your service. There we shall eat of the offerings and Passover sacrifices which will be acceptably placed upon your altar. We shall sing a new hymn of praise to you for our redemption and for our liberation. Praised are you, Adonai, who has redeemed Israel.

Praised are you, Adonai, our God, sovereign of the universe, who has created the fruit of the vine.

Rachtzah

Finally, we begin the Passover meal, the third section or "third cup" of the Seder. Storytelling leads into communal eating, because on Passover, "Jews eat history."

On Passover, the traditional handwashing is often done seated, while volunteers bring around a pitcher, a towel and a basin to each participant. After pouring water over each hand, say the blessing.

Wash hands while reciting the traditional blessing for washing the hands:

בָּרוּךְ אַתָּה יי אֱלֹהֵינוּ מֶלֶךְ הָעוֹלָם, אֲשֶׁר קִדְּשָׁנוּ בְּמִצְוֹתָיו וְצִוָּנוּ עַל נְטִילַת יָדָיִם.

Baruch atah Adonai Eloheinu melech ha-olam, asher kid'shanu b'mitzvotav, v'tzivanu al n'tilat yadayim.

Praised are you, Adonai, Lord our God, Ruler of the universe, who has taught us the way of holiness through commandments, commanding us to wash our hands.

With or Without Salt?	With or Without Charoset?
Rabbi Yose Karo opinion on the custom of dipping the matzah in salt during the Passover seder is that it is a way of remembering the sacrifices of the past and of adding flavor and enjoyment to the seder meal.	Rabbi Abraham ben Ezra's opinion on the custom of dipping the matzah in charoset during the Passover seder is that it is a way of recalling the hardship and slavery of the past and of adding flavor and enjoyment to the seder meal.
But other Rabbis protested that matzah is the bread of poverty and should be eaten plain without any seasoning. Ultimately, it is up to you for which of the two you believe holds true.	But other Rabbis protested that matzah is the bread of poverty and should be eaten plain without any seasoning. Ultimately, it is up to you for which of the two you believe holds true.

Motzi Matzahh

Eating the Matzah

This is the one time during Pesach in which one is obligated to eat matzah. It must be plain matzah without eggs or other ingredients that might enrich this bread of poverty.

Take the three matzot in hand. Make sure the middle one is broken and the others are still whole. Recite the usual blessing for all forms of bread – the "the motzi" – and the special blessing for matzah – "al acheelat matzah."

Say the two blessings over the matzah:

בָּרוּךְ אַתָּה יי אלוהינו מֶלֶךְ הָעוֹלָם הַמּוֹצִיא לֶחֶם מִן הָאָרֶץ.

Baruch atah Adonai, Eloheinu melech ha-olam, hamotzi lechem min ha-aretz.

Praised are you, Adonai, Lord our God, Ruler of the universe, who provides sustenance from the earth.

בָּרוּךְ אַתָּה יי אלוהינו מֶלֶךְ הָעוֹלָם, אֲשֶׁר קִדְּשָׁנוּ בְּמִצְוֹתָיו וְצִנָּנוּ עַל אֲכִילַת מַצָּה.

Baruch atah Adonai, Eloheinu melech ha-olam, asher kid'shanu b'mitzvotav v'tzivanu al achilat matzahh.

Praised are you, Adonai, Lord our God, Ruler of the universe, who has taught us the way of holiness through commandments, commanding us to eat matzah.

Take and Eat from the top and middle matzah, while reclining (left). Save the third matzah for the Hillel sandwich.

You may dip the matzah in salt or charoset.

One Should eat an amount equivalent to at least 1/3 – 2/3 of a standard machine-made matzah.

31

Maror

The Maror step of the seder is a time for eating bitter herbs and for reflecting on the symbolism and meaning of this special food as an embodiment of the bitterness of slavery. It is an important part of the seder experience and helps to bring to life the themes of liberation and freedom that are central to the seder.

Dip it in charoset (but not so much that it eradicates the bitter taste). Recite the blessing, eat and savor the maror but **do not recline!** Reclining is a custom of the free, while maror and charoset remind us of persecution.

Dip bitter herbs in charoset and say:

בָּרוּךְ אַתָּה יי אֱלֹהֵינוּ מֶלֶךְ הָעוֹלָם, אֲשֶׁר קִדְּשָׁנוּ בְּמִצְוֹתָיו וְצִוָּנוּ עַל אֲכִילַת מָרוֹר.

Baruch atah Adonai Eloheinu melech ha-olam, asher kid'shanu b'mitzvotav v'tzivanu al achilat maror.

Praised are you, Adonai, Lord our God, Ruler of the universe, who has taught us the way of holiness through commandments, commanding us to eat the bitter herb.

Khorech

Take the third, bottom matzah, and prepare a sandwich of matzah, maror and charoset. Eat it while reclining to the left.

זֵכֶר לְמִקְדָּשׁ כְּהִלֵּל.

כֵּן עָשָׂה הִלֵּל בִּזְמַן שֶׁבֵּית הַמִּקְדָּשׁ הָיָה קַיָּם: הָיָה כּוֹרֵךְ מַצָּה וּמָרוֹר וְאוֹכֵל בְּיַחַד, לְקַיֵּים מַה שֶׁנֶּאֱמַר: עַל מַצּוֹת וּמְרֹרִים יֹאכְלֻהוּ.

Zeicher l'mikdash k'hileil. Kein asah hileil bizman shebeit hamikdash hayah kayam. Hayah koreich pesach, matzahh, u-maror v'ocheil b'yachad. L'kayeim mah shene-emar. "Al matzot um'rorim yochlu-hu."

We have just eaten matzah and maror separately. However, in the days of the Temple, Hillel, the head of the Sanhedrin, used to bind into one sandwich: Pesach lamb, matzah and maror. He ate them all together in order to observe the las: *" You shall eat it on matzot and maror."* (Number 9:11)
Eating the sandwich tonight reminds us of the Temple sacrifice in Jerusalem as performed according to Hillel.

(All:) In memory of Pesach in the Temple as Hillel used to celebrate it.

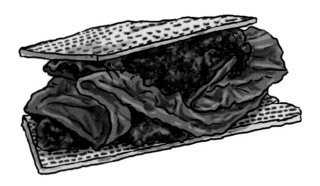

And now it's time to eat!

Set aside your Haggadot and enjoy a wonderful dinner.

Eating the Hidden Afikoman

The Afikoman, the other half of the middle matzah which was hidden at the beginning of the Seder, must now be eaten. It is specifically last such that its taste lingers as the last food eaten at the Seder.

The leaders of the Passover seder pretend to be upset because the children have "stolen" the Afikoman, which is a piece of matzah that is set aside to be eaten later in the seder. They have to bargain to get it back.

After everyone has finished dessert, a piece of Afikoman mixed with more matzah is given out.

Even though people might be full, it is important to end the seder by eating matzah while lying down. This is because matzah has already been eaten at the beginning of the seder, and the Afikoman is a substitute for the lamb that was once eaten at the end of the seder after people were full.

<u>After the Afikoman is eaten, no more food or drink is allowed except for the third and fourth cups of wine.</u>

Bircat Hamazon

After the Meal we thank God for the food that has been provided and for the many blessings that God has given to the Jewish people. These blessings are recited over the third cup of wine which we pour now and drink at the end of Barech.

בָּרוּךְ אַתָּה יְיָ, אֱלֹהֵינוּ מֶלֶךְ הָעוֹלָם, הַזָּן אֶת הָעוֹלָם כֻּלּוֹ בְּטוּבוֹ בְּחֵן בְּחֶסֶד וּבְרַחֲמִים. הוּא נוֹתֵן לֶחֶם לְכָל בָּשָׂר כִּי לְעוֹלָם חַסְדּוֹ. וּבְטוּבוֹ הַגָּדוֹל תָּמִיד לֹא חָסַר לָנוּ, וְאַל יֶחְסַר לָנוּ מָזוֹן לְעוֹלָם וָעֶד. בַּעֲבוּר שְׁמוֹ הַגָּדוֹל כִּי הוּא אֵל זָן וּמְפַרְנֵס לַכֹּל וּמֵטִיב לַכֹּל וּמֵכִין מָזוֹן לְכָל בְּרִיּוֹתָיו אֲשֶׁר בָּרָא. **בָּרוּךְ אַתָּה יְיָ, הַזָּן אֶת הַכֹּל.**

Ba-ruch a-tah A-do-nai, E-lo-hei-nu Me-lech Ha-o-lam, Ha-zan et ha-o-lam ku-lo, b'tu-vo, b'chein b'che-sed uv-ra-cha-mim, hu no-tein le-chem l'chawl ba-sar, ki l'o-lam chas-do. Uv-tu-vo ha-ga-dol i-ma-nu, ta-mid lo cha-seir la-nu, v'al yech-sar la-nu, ma-zon l'o-lam va-ed. Ba-a-vur sh'mo ha-ga-dol, ki hu Eil zan um-far-neis la-kol, u-mei-tiv la-kol, u-mei-chin ma-zon l'chawl b'ri-yo-tav a-sher ba-ra. Ka-a-mur: Po-tei-ach et ya-de-cha, u-mas-bi-a l'chawl chai ra-tson. Ba-ruch a-tah A-do-nai, ha-zan et ha-kol. (A-mein.)

Blessed are you, Adonai our God, Sovereign of the universe, who nourishes the whole world. Your kindness endures forever. May we never be in want of food, for God provides for all the creatures which God has created. **Blessed are You, Adonai, who feeds all.**

Third Cup of Wine

We conclude the Blessing over the meal by drinking the third cup, the cup of Blessing, while reclining to the left.

בָּרוּךְ אַתָּה יְיָ, אֱלֹהֵינוּ מֶלֶךְ הָעוֹלָם, בּוֹרֵא פְּרִי הַגָּפֶן.

Blessed are You, Lord our God, King of the universe, who creates the fruit of the vine.

Cup of Elijah

Pour a large cup of wine in honor of Elijah.

Open the door for Elijah.

The Cup of Elijah is a cup of wine that is set aside during the Passover seder and is not consumed. It is symbolic of the prophet Elijah, who is believed to be a messenger of God and who is associated with the coming of the Messiah.

According to tradition, Elijah will come to announce the coming of the Messiah and to usher in a time of peace and prosperity for the Jewish people. The Cup of Elijah is a way of inviting Elijah to come to the seder and to join in the celebration.

During the seder, the door of the home is traditionally left open to symbolize the welcoming of Elijah. The Cup of Elijah is placed on the seder table and is filled with wine. It is not consumed during the seder, but is left as an offering for Elijah.

The Cup of Elijah is a powerful symbol in the Passover seder and represents the hope for redemption and the coming of the Messiah. It is a way of inviting Elijah to join in the celebration and of expressing the belief that one day he will come to bring about a time of peace and prosperity for the Jewish people.

אֵלִיָּהוּ הַנָּבִיא, אֵלִיָּהוּ הַתִּשְׁבִּי,
אֵלִיָּהוּ, אֵלִיָּהוּ, אֵלִיָּהוּ הַגִּלְעָדִי,
בִּמְהֵרָה בְיָמֵינוּ יָבוֹא אֵלֵינוּ
עִם מָשִׁיחַ בֶּן דָּוִד, עִם מָשִׁיחַ בֶּן דָּוִד.

Eliyahu ha-navi, Eliyahu ha-Tishbi,
Eliyahu (3x) ha-Giladi.
Bimheirah v'yameinu, yavo ei-leinu
im Mashiach ben David (2x)

Elijah, the prophet; Elijiah, the Tishbite; Elijah, of Gilead! Soon, in our days, may he come together with the Messiah, the son of David.

Keep Elijah's Cup on the table.

Close the door and be seated.

Fourth Cup of Wine

The 2nd half of Hallel is traditionally read before the 4th cup. It is a long liturgy that has been omitted. For those who wish to read it please refer to a traditional Haggadah.

Hallel is a series of prayers and Psalms that are traditionally recited during the Passover seder and other Jewish festivals. The Hallel consists of two parts: the Great Hallel and the Minor Hallel.

The Great Hallel consists of Psalms 113-118, and is recited in full during the Passover seder. These Psalms praise God and express thanks for the many blessings that God has given to the Jewish people.

The Minor Hallel consists of Psalms 146-150, and is traditionally recited in full on Jewish holidays. These Psalms also praise God and express thanks for the many blessings that God has given to the Jewish people.

The Hallel is an important part of the Passover seder and is a way of expressing gratitude and appreciation for the blessings that God has given to the Jewish people. It is a time for praising God and for thanking Him for His goodness and mercy.

Raise the fourth cup of wine, recite the blessing over it and recline to the left while drinking.

בָּרוּךְ אַתָּה יְיָ, אֱלֹהֵינוּ מֶלֶךְ הָעוֹלָם, בּוֹרֵא פְּרִי הַגָּפֶן.

Blessed are You, Lord our God, King of the universe, who creates the fruit of the vine.

Echad Mi Yodei'a
Who Knows One?

אֶחָד מִי יוֹדֵעַ

This song began to appear in Haggadot during the 16th century. Since the song is popular among children, we substituted "mothers and fathers" for "matriarchs and patriarchs" to facilitate the singing.

Despite the song's fun question and answer format, we should be mindful of its title. This expresses the belief that God is One, which is central to Judaism and was reinforced during the time of Passover.

Who knows one? I know one.
One is our God in heaven and on earth.

אֶחָד מִי יוֹדֵעַ? אֶחָד אֲנִי יוֹדֵעַ: אֶחָד אֱלֹהֵינוּ שֶׁבַּשָּׁמַיִם וּבָאָרֶץ.

Who knows two? I know two.
Two are the tablets of the Covenant. One is our God in heaven and on earth.

שְׁנַיִם מִי יוֹדֵעַ? שְׁנַיִם אֲנִי יוֹדֵעַ: שְׁנֵי לֻחוֹת הַבְּרִית, אֶחָד אֱלֹהֵינוּ שֶׁבַּשָּׁמַיִם וּבָאָרֶץ.

Who knows three? I know three.
Three are the fathers. Two are the tablets of the Covenant. One is our God in heaven and on earth.

שְׁלֹשָׁה מִי יוֹדֵעַ? שְׁלֹשָׁה אֲנִי יוֹדֵעַ: שְׁלֹשָׁה אָבוֹת, שְׁנֵי לֻחוֹת הַבְּרִית, אֶחָד אֱלֹהֵינוּ שֶׁבַּשָּׁמַיִם וּבָאָרֶץ.

Who knows four? I know four.
Four are the mothers. Three are the fathers. Two are the tablets of the Covenant. One is our God in heaven and on earth.

אַרְבַּע מִי יוֹדֵעַ? אַרְבַּע אֲנִי יוֹדֵעַ: אַרְבַּע אִמָּהוֹת, שְׁלֹשָׁה אָבוֹת, שְׁנֵי לֻחוֹת הַבְּרִית, אֶחָד אֱלֹהֵינוּ שֶׁבַּשָּׁמַיִם וּבָאָרֶץ.

Who knows five? I know five.
Five are the books of the Torah. Four are the mothers. Three are the fathers. Two are the tablets of the Covenant. One is our God in heaven and on earth.

חֲמִשָּׁה מִי יוֹדֵעַ? חֲמִשָּׁה אֲנִי יוֹדֵעַ: חֲמִשָּׁה חוּמְשֵׁי תוֹרָה, אַרְבַּע אִמָּהוֹת, שְׁלֹשָׁה אָבוֹת, שְׁנֵי לֻחוֹת הַבְּרִית, אֶחָד אֱלֹהֵינוּ שֶׁבַּשָּׁמַיִם וּבָאָרֶץ.

Who knows six? I know six.
Six are the sections of the Mishnah. Five are the books of the Torah. Four are the mothers. Three are the fathers. Two are the tablets of the Covenant. One is our God in heaven and on earth.

שִׁשָּׁה מִי יוֹדֵעַ? שִׁשָּׁה אֲנִי יוֹדֵעַ: שִׁשָּׁה סִדְרֵי מִשְׁנָה, חֲמִשָּׁה חוּמְשֵׁי תוֹרָה, אַרְבַּע אִמָּהוֹת, שְׁלֹשָׁה אָבוֹת, שְׁנֵי לֻחוֹת הַבְּרִית, אֶחָד אֱלֹהֵינוּ שֶׁבַּשָּׁמַיִם וּבָאָרֶץ.

Who knows seven? I know seven.
Seven are the days of the week. Six are the sections of the Mishnah. Five are the books of the Torah. Four are the mothers. Three are the fathers. Two are the tablets of the Covenant. One is our God in heaven and on earth.

שִׁבְעָה מִי יוֹדֵעַ? שִׁבְעָה אֲנִי יוֹדֵעַ: שִׁבְעָה יְמֵי שַׁבַּתָּא, שִׁשָּׁה סִדְרֵי מִשְׁנָה, חֲמִשָּׁה חוּמְשֵׁי תוֹרָה, אַרְבַּע אִמָּהוֹת, שְׁלֹשָׁה אָבוֹת, שְׁנֵי לֻחוֹת הַבְּרִית, אֶחָד אֱלֹהֵינוּ שֶׁבַּשָּׁמַיִם וּבָאָרֶץ.

Who knows eight? I know eight.
Eight are the days to circumcision. Seven are the days of the week. Six are the sections of the Mishnah. Five are the books of the Torah. Four are the mothers. Three are the fathers. Two are the tablets of the Covenant. One is our God in heaven and on earth.

שְׁמוֹנָה מִי יוֹדֵעַ? שְׁמוֹנָה אֲנִי יוֹדֵעַ: שְׁמוֹנָה יְמֵי מִילָה, שִׁבְעָה יְמֵי שַׁבַּתָּא, שִׁשָּׁה סִדְרֵי מִשְׁנָה, חֲמִשָּׁה חוּמְשֵׁי תוֹרָה, אַרְבַּע אִמָּהוֹת, שְׁלֹשָׁה אָבוֹת, שְׁנֵי לֻחוֹת הַבְּרִית, אֶחָד אֱלֹהֵינוּ שֶׁבַּשָּׁמַיִם וּבָאָרֶץ.

Who knows nine? I know nine.
Nine are the months to childbirth. Eight are the days to circumcision. Seven are the days of the week. Six are the sections of the Mishnah. Five are the books of the Torah. Four are the mothers. Three are the fathers. Two are the tablets of the Covenant. One is our God in heaven and on earth.

תִּשְׁעָה מִי יוֹדֵעַ? תִּשְׁעָה אֲנִי יוֹדֵעַ: תִּשְׁעָה
יַרְחֵי לֵדָה, שְׁמוֹנָה יְמֵי מִילָה, שִׁבְעָה יְמֵי שַׁבַּתָּא,
שִׁשָּׁה סִדְרֵי מִשְׁנָה, חֲמִשָּׁה חוּמְשֵׁי תוֹרָה,
אַרְבַּע אִמָּהוֹת, שְׁלֹשָׁה אָבוֹת, שְׁנֵי לֻחוֹת הַבְּרִית,
אֶחָד אֱלֹהֵינוּ שֶׁבַּשָּׁמַיִם וּבָאָרֶץ.

Who knows ten? I know ten.
Ten are the Ten Commandments. Nine are the months to childbirth. Eight are the days to circumcision. Seven are the days of the week. Six are the sections of the Mishnah. Five are the books of the Torah. Four are the mothers. Three are the fathers. Two are the tablets of the Covenant. One is our God in heaven and on earth.

עֲשָׂרָה מִי יוֹדֵעַ? עֲשָׂרָה אֲנִי יוֹדֵעַ: עֲשָׂרָה דִבְּרַיָּא,
תִּשְׁעָה יַרְחֵי לֵדָה, שְׁמוֹנָה יְמֵי מִילָה, שִׁבְעָה יְמֵי
שַׁבַּתָּא, שִׁשָּׁה סִדְרֵי מִשְׁנָה, חֲמִשָּׁה חוּמְשֵׁי תוֹרָה,
אַרְבַּע אִמָּהוֹת, שְׁלֹשָׁה אָבוֹת, שְׁנֵי לֻחוֹת הַבְּרִית,
אֶחָד אֱלֹהֵינוּ שֶׁבַּשָּׁמַיִם וּבָאָרֶץ.

Who knows eleven? I know eleven.
Eleven are the stars in Joseph's dream. Ten are the Ten Commandments. Nine are the months to childbirth. Eight are the days to circumcision. Seven are the days of the week. Six are the sections of the Mishnah. Five are the books of the Torah. Four are the mothers. Three are the fathers. Two are the tablets of the Covenant. One is our God in heaven and on earth.

אַחַד עָשָׂר מִי יוֹדֵעַ? אַחַד עָשָׂר אֲנִי יוֹדֵעַ: אַחַד עָשָׂר
כּוֹכְבַיָּא, עֲשָׂרָה דִבְּרַיָּא, תִּשְׁעָה יַרְחֵי לֵדָה, שְׁמוֹנָה
יְמֵי מִילָה, שִׁבְעָה יְמֵי שַׁבַּתָּא, שִׁשָּׁה סִדְרֵי מִשְׁנָה,
חֲמִשָּׁה חוּמְשֵׁי תוֹרָה, אַרְבַּע אִמָּהוֹת, שְׁלֹשָׁה אָבוֹת,
שְׁנֵי לֻחוֹת הַבְּרִית, אֶחָד אֱלֹהֵינוּ שֶׁבַּשָּׁמַיִם וּבָאָרֶץ.

Who knows twelve? I know twelve.
Twelve are the tribes of Israel. Eleven are the stars in Joseph's dream. Ten are the Ten Commandments. Nine are the months to childbirth. Eight are the days to circumcision. Seven are the days of the week. Six are the sections of the Mishnah. Five are the books of the Torah. Four are the mothers. Three are the fathers. Two are the tablets of the Covenant. One is our God in heaven and on earth.

שְׁנֵים עָשָׂר מִי יוֹדֵעַ? שְׁנֵים עָשָׂר אֲנִי יוֹדֵעַ: שְׁנֵים
עָשָׂר שִׁבְטַיָּא, אַחַד עָשָׂר כּוֹכְבַיָּא, עֲשָׂרָה דִבְּרַיָּא,
תִּשְׁעָה יַרְחֵי לֵדָה, שְׁמוֹנָה יְמֵי מִילָה, שִׁבְעָה יְמֵי
שַׁבַּתָּא, שִׁשָּׁה סִדְרֵי מִשְׁנָה, חֲמִשָּׁה חוּמְשֵׁי תוֹרָה,
אַרְבַּע אִמָּהוֹת, שְׁלֹשָׁה אָבוֹת, שְׁנֵי לֻחוֹת הַבְּרִית,
אֶחָד אֱלֹהֵינוּ שֶׁבַּשָּׁמַיִם וּבָאָרֶץ.

Who knows thirteen? I know thirteen.
Thirteen are the attributes of God. Twelve are the tribes of Israel. Eleven are the stars in Joseph's dream. Ten are the Ten Commandments. Nine are the months to childbirth. Eight are the days to circumcision. Seven are the days of the week. Six are the sections of the Mishnah. Five are the books of the Torah. Four are the mothers. Three are the fathers. Two are the tablets of the Covenant. One is our God in heaven and on earth.

שְׁלֹשָׁה עָשָׂר מִי יוֹדֵעַ? שְׁלֹשָׁה עָשָׂר אֲנִי יוֹדֵעַ: שְׁלֹשָׁה
עָשָׂר מִדַּיָּא, שְׁנֵים עָשָׂר שִׁבְטַיָּא, אַחַד עָשָׂר כּוֹכְבַיָּא,
עֲשָׂרָה דִבְּרַיָּא, תִּשְׁעָה יַרְחֵי לֵדָה, שְׁמוֹנָה יְמֵי מִילָה,
שִׁבְעָה יְמֵי שַׁבַּתָּא, שִׁשָּׁה סִדְרֵי מִשְׁנָה, חֲמִשָּׁה חוּמְשֵׁי
תוֹרָה, אַרְבַּע אִמָּהוֹת, שְׁלֹשָׁה אָבוֹת, שְׁנֵי לֻחוֹת
הַבְּרִית, אֶחָד אֱלֹהֵינוּ שֶׁבַּשָּׁמַיִם וּבָאָרֶץ.

Nirtza

The Nirtza step of the Passover seder is the conclusion of the seder, in which the participants express their desire to participate in another seder in the future.

At the end of the seder, the leader of the seder will typically say the words **"Next year in Jerusalem,"** which expresses the hope and desire to be able to celebrate the Passover seder in the city of Jerusalem in the future.

The Nirtza is a way of bringing the seder to a close and of looking ahead to the next year's seder with joy and anticipation.

חֲסַל סִדּוּר פֶּסַח כְּהִלְכָתוֹ, כְּכָל מִשְׁפָּטוֹ וְחֻקָתוֹ. כַּאֲשֶׁר זָכִינוּ לְסַדֵּר אוֹתוֹ. כֵּן נִזְכֶּה לַעֲשׂוֹתוֹ. זָךְ שׁוֹכֵן מְעוֹנָה, קוֹמֵם קְהַל עֲדַת מִי מָנָה. בְּקָרוֹב נַהֵל נִטְעֵי כַנָּה. פְּדוּיִם לְצִיּוֹן בְּרִנָּה.

Chasal sidur pesach k'hilchato, k'chol mishpato v'chukato. Ka-asher zachinu l'sadeir oto, kein nizkeh la-asoto. Zach shochein m'onah, komeim k'hal adat mi manah. B'karov naheil nitei chanah, p'duyim l'tzion b'rinah.

The Passover Seder is concluded, according to each traditional detail with all its laws and customs. As we have been privileged to celebrate this Seder, so may we one day celebrate it in Jerusalem. Pure One who dwells in the high places, support your People countless in number. May you soon redeem all your People joyfully in Zion.

לְשָׁנָה הַבָּאָה בִּירוּשָׁלָיִם.

L'shana Haba'ah b'Y'rushalayim

Next Year in Jerusalem!

41

Made in the USA
Middletown, DE
13 March 2023

26643736R00024